Vinegar Solutions

Money Saving, Green Ideas for Cleaning, Cooking and Health

M.B. Ryther

Revised Edition

Copyright © 2012, 2016 M.B. Ryther

ISBN-13: 978-1475276053

ISBN-10: 1475276052

Disclaimer

This book is not intended as a substitute for the medical advice of physicians. The reader should regularly consult a physician in matters relating to his/her health and particularly with respect to any symptoms that may require diagnosis or medical attention.

CONTENTS

VINEGAR, WHO KNEW?

The Multi-Purpose Product

Most of us know that vinegar will clean a coffeemaker and shine a window. And, of course, everyone knows that it's great on salads. But did you know that it can also clean your jewelry, kill your weeds, keep fleas off your dog, and deodorize a room? And you may not know this either: Scientific studies conducted within the last decade show vinegar to be effective in helping people with type 2 diabetes control their blood glucose levels.

The truth is, vinegar can do all that and more. In fact, vinegar can do so much around the house that there may be little need for that stash of cleaning products under the sink. Unlike many of those products, vinegar is non-abrasive, so it's safe to use on even the most delicate glassware. It's also non-toxic, allowing it to be used harmlessly around kids and pets. Without a doubt, there are few products available today that are as versatile as vinegar, as effective, as safe, and as cheap.

Vinegar Basics

Vinegar (from the French word *vinaigre*, "sour wine") is mostly water containing an active ingredient of acetic acid. It is made from a variety of raw materials such as fruits, grains, sugars, syrups, and wine, which are fermented to form ethyl alcohol. To this is added acetic acid-forming bacteria which converts the alcohol to vinegar. The many varieties of vinegar (distilled white, apple cider, wine, malt, and garlic, among others) are determined by the raw materials used, as well as by the fermenting and distilling processes.

Vinegar History

Vinegar has been around for a long time. The ancient Babylonians were the first to turn wine into vinegar, sometime around 5,000 B.C. The idea of "soured wine" eventually passed down to the Greeks and Romans, whose literature abounds with passages reflecting its popularity. Hippocrates, for example, used vinegar as an antibiotic. Helen of Troy bathed in it as a way of relaxing. And Cleopatra supposedly dissolved her pearls in vinegar to win a bet with Mark Antony that she could consume a fortune in a single meal.

By 1,000 B.C. many Oriental cultures had discovered the food preserving quality of vinegar and added spices to improve its taste. During the Black Plague of the Middle Ages, thieves poured vinegar over their hands before robbing the dead to ward off germs. And during the seventeenth century, Europeans commonly used vinegar as a deodorant and deodorizer; the aristocracy would often be seen holding vinegar-scented sponges to their noses to mask the smell of offensive street sewage. In American history, vinegar was reportedly used during the Civil War to treat and prevent scurvy, and later used in World War I to treat wounds of soldiers.

A Few Recommendations

- Unless stated otherwise, simple distilled white vinegar of the least expensive variety will work just fine for most of the ideas in this book. Save the more expensive gourmet vinegars for your palette.

- Get a couple of spray bottles to keep solutions of vinegar and water – or straight undiluted vinegar – handy in your kitchen, your laundry room, your garage, or wherever you keep your cleaning supplies.

- Don't assume that mixing vinegar with one of your other cleansers will enhance that product's effectiveness. It could be dangerous. The acetic acid in vinegar when mixed with some lavatory bowl cleaners, for example, produces a deadly chlorine gas.

- Don't get too hung up on exact measurements, even though you will see suggested ratios in many of the tips printed here. They are just that, *suggestions*. Even different vinegar makers and other published household tipsters will sometimes differ on whether to use a $1/2$ cup vs. whole cup, etc. Use the given suggestions as a guideline at first, and adjust when and if you feel it's necessary. Don't be afraid of using your instinct. A "splash" in many cases is just as good as a measured tablespoon.

Now, go into the kitchen and grab that bottle – the vinegar bottle, that is!

KITCHEN HINTS

Clean the coffeemaker

Fill the pot with water and a cup of vinegar. Run through the normal cycle and let stand until it cools. Repeat if it's been awhile since last cleaned. Then rinse with a cycle of plain water.

Deodorize the kitchen drain

Pour a cup of vinegar down the drain once a week. Let it stand for 30 minutes and then flush with tap water.

Clean and deodorize the garbage disposal

Make ice cubes out of a cup of vinegar and enough water to fill the ice tray. Then feed the cubes down the disposal. After grinding, run cold water through for about a minute.

Eliminate onion odor from hands

Rub vinegar on your fingers before and after slicing onions to cut the smell.

Remove fruit stains from your hands

Simply rub them in vinegar.

Disinfect fresh produce

Fill your sink with a gallon of cold water and add a cup of white or apple cider vinegar. Rinse your fruits and vegetables in this solution to get rid of dirt, germs, pesticides, and insects.

Clean the drainboard

Get rid of hard water stains by pouring vinegar over the board (or soaking it in the sink if easier) and letting it set overnight. Rub the stains off in the morning.

Clean and disinfect cutting boards

Wipe with full-strength vinegar.

Clean the microwave

Boil a solution of 1/4 cup vinegar and 1 cup of water in the microwave. Will loosen splattered-on food and deodorize.

Get stains and odors out of pots

Fill pot with a solution of vinegar and water. Boil until stains loosen and can be washed away.

Unclog a drain

Pour a handful of baking soda down the drain and add a 1/2 cup of vinegar. Then rinse with cold water.

Freshen a lunchbox

Soak a piece of bread in vinegar and let it set in the lunchbox overnight.

Clean a thermos

Fill with 1/4 cup of vinegar and warm water. Add some uncooked rice to help rub off grime. Put the lid on and shake vigorously. Rinse out and allow to air dry.

Clean the refrigerator

Use a solution of equal parts vinegar and water to wash out grime and food odors.

Clean and deodorize jars

Eliminate odors from those mayonnaise, peanut butter, and mustard jars you save by rinsing them with vinegar when empty.

Clean a teapot

Boil a mixture of water and vinegar in the teapot. Then wipe away the dirt and grime easily.

Get rid of dishwasher spots

Add a 1/2 cup of vinegar to the second rinse.

Clean the dishwasher

Place a cup of vinegar on the bottom rack, and then, with no other dishes in the washer, run a complete cycle. Do this once a month to reduce soap buildup on the inner mechanisms.

Make drinking glasses sparkle

Add a cup of vinegar to a sink of warm, soapy water and wash glasses by hand to remove cloudiness and spots. (Works well with china and fine glassware too.)

Clean stainless steel and chrome

Remove spots from stainless steel by wiping with a vinegar-dampened cloth.

Cut grease and odors on dishes

Add a splash or more of vinegar to hot, soapy wash water.

Remove coffee and tea stains from china

Use equal parts vinegar and salt to loosen and remove stains from china cups.

Remove tarnish from copper pots and utensils

Brush a thin coating of vinegar over the tarnish and apply an even coating of salt. Then rub away the tarnish with a dry cloth and rinse in hot water.

Clean faucets and taps

To remove tough mineral deposits on faucets, wrap them in cloths or paper towels soaked in vinegar. Cover the area in plastic wrap to prevent evaporation. Wait an hour or two, and then wash away the sediment with a soft brush or cloth. Rinse and dry.

Get rid of cooking smells

Let simmer on the stovetop a small pot of equal parts vinegar and water.

LAUNDRY HELPS

Unclog the steam iron

Pour equal amounts of vinegar and water into the iron's water chamber. Turn to "steam" and leave the iron on for five minutes in an upright position. Then unplug and allow to cool. Any loose particles should come out when you empty the water.

Clean a scorched iron plate

Make a paste of salt and heated vinegar. Rub onto the surface of a cool iron to remove dark or burned-on stains.

Remove starch on an iron

Wipe the plate of a cold iron with vinegar.

Iron out dryer wrinkles

Get rid of wrinkles caused by a too-hot or too-long dryer cycle by ironing over the wrinkles with a "pressing cloth" dampened with vinegar. (Works for hemline creases too.)

Maintain your washer

Once a month, pour a cup of vinegar into the washer (without any added clothes) and run it through a normal cycle to remove unwanted soap residue.

Brighten and soften fabrics

Add up to one cup of vinegar to the rinse cycle to break up soap buildup, thereby brightening and softening the fabrics.

Put fluff in the blankets

Add two cups of vinegar in the rinse cycle for loads of cotton and wool blankets.

Keep clothes static-and-lint free

Yep, you guessed it. Add a cup of vinegar to the rinse cycle.

Keep colors from running

Immerse clothes in full-strength vinegar before washing.

Fix a shrunken sweater

Boil a shrunken wool garment in one part vinegar and two parts water for 25 minutes. Reshape the garment and allow to air dry.

Whiten socks

For the most bleach-resistant, grime-laden socks, try this: In a large pot, add a cup of vinegar to 1 1/2 quarts of water and bring to a boil. Then pour the piping hot solution into a bucket, toss in the dingy sock, and let them soak overnight. The next day, wash as usual.

Take grease off of suede

Dip a toothbrush in vinegar and gently brush over the grease spot. Allow to dry.

Remove tough stains

Rub vinegar gently over wine, cola, fruit, jam, mustard, coffee, deodorant, and perspiration stains. Then wash as usual.

Get the smoke smell out of clothes (without washing)

Add a cup of vinegar to a bathtub of hot water. Hang clothes above the steam.

Soften drapes

Add a few drops of vinegar to the rinse cycle when laundering drapes or synthetic curtains to soften and reduce static.

Pamper your nylons

Add a splash of vinegar to two quarts of wash water to make nylons gleam and last longer.

Remove salt and water stains from boots and shoes

Wipe with full-strength vinegar to remove salt and water stains. Polish if desired.

Clean black patent leather shoes

Wipe with a solution of vinegar and water to remove spots.

Prevent clothesline freeze

Wipe clothesline with a vinegar-dampened cloth to prevent clothes from sticking to the line in cold weather.

BATHROOM SOLUTIONS

Clean plastic shower curtains

Wash in the machine along with a bath towel. Then add a cup of vinegar to the rinse cycle. Will make the curtains soft and pliable, as well as remove soap and grime buildup.

Clean a removable shower head

Soak in a container of vinegar overnight. Will unclog holes due to mineral deposits and remove corrosion.

Clean a fixed shower head (or faucet)

Wrap a vinegar-saturated cloth around the shower head or faucet and leave on overnight. Wipe away the grime the next day. Alternatively, fill a plastic bag with undiluted vinegar and attach it around the shower head with a rubber band or tape. Leave it overnight or check it after a few hours to see if it makes a difference.

Shine your fixtures

Dampen a sponge or cloth with full-strength vinegar and wipe down chrome, stainless steel, ceramic, or plastic fixtures. Polish with a soft cloth.

Clean the toilet bowl

Use full-strength vinegar and a sturdy brush to remove stubborn stains. Deodorize the bowl by pouring in 3 cups of vinegar and letting it sit for 30-60 minutes before flushing.

Clean tile grout

Use full-strength vinegar and a brush to clean grout and remove mildew.

Clean tub and tile surfaces

Wipe away rings and soap film with full-strength vinegar. Rinse with water. For tough tub rings, fill the tub with hot water (enough to cover the rings) and mix in three cups of full-strength vinegar. Let it sit for four hours. The ring should wipe away fairly easily after that.

Clean and polish glass shower doors

Wipe with a vinegar and water solution to make doors sparkle.

Unstiffen a toothbrush

Soak in hot vinegar for 30 minutes and rinse out.

Clean combs and hairbrushes

First, remove as much loose hair as possible from the combs and brushes. Then combine 2 teaspoons of shampoo and 1/4 cup of white vinegar in a clean sink or bucket filled with warm/hot water. Submerge the combs and brushes in the solution allow to soak for 10 to 15 minutes. Afterwards, rinse with water and remove any lingering hairs and crud with tweezers or toothpicks. Allow to dry.

ALL AROUND THE HOUSE

Wash your windows

Spray on a solution of equal parts vinegar and water. Polish with newspaper for a streak-free shine.

Remove tape or sticky residue on windows

Rub sticky area with warm vinegar, allow to soak in, and then peel or scrub off.

Clean no-wax floors

Make them shine with a solution of 1/2 cup of vinegar and a 1/2 gallon of warm water.

Clean indoor and outdoor carpet

Mix a gallon of water, a cup of vinegar and just enough dish soap to make sudsy. Brush it on the carpeting and blot dry with towels.

Clean brick floors and walls

Mop or brush them with a cup of vinegar mixed into a gallon of hot water.

Clean varnished or natural woodwork

Wipe down with a cloth moistened lightly with a solution of water and a few drops of vinegar.

Remove old glue from wood

Wipe area with hot vinegar.

Clean wood furniture

Make a solution of 1 tablespoon of vinegar to 1 quart of water. Wipe down furniture and dry with a lint-free cloth.

Peel off wallpaper

Spray the wallpaper with a solution of equal parts vinegar and water until it's saturated. Wait a few minutes and then scrape off.

Clean mini blinds

Make a solution of equal parts vinegar and hot water. Put on a cotton gardening glove, moisten your fingers in the vinegar solution, and slide your fingers across both slides of the slat. (Periodically wash off your glove in some clean water.)

Polish up the paneling

Combine 1 pint of warm water, 4 tablespoons of white vinegar, and 2 tablespoons of olive oil in a container. Cover tightly and mix together with a few vigorous shakes. Wipe down paneling with a cloth soaked in the mixture, then polish with a dry cloth.

Restore luster to leather furniture

In a spray bottle combine equals parts vinegar and boiled linseed oil. Shake it up to mix. Then spray it on your chair or other piece of furniture and spread evenly with a cloth. Let it sit for a few minutes and then rub if off with a clean cloth.

Cover up scratches in wood furniture

Mix vinegar and iodine together in a small container and apply to scratch with a small artist's brush. For darker woods, use more iodine; for lighter woods, use more vinegar.

Remove decals from surfaces

Brush with a couple of coats of vinegar. Allow to soak in. Decals should easily wash off after several minutes.

Clean stainless steel and chrome fixtures

Spray or wipe on a light coating of full-strength vinegar and polish to desired shine.

Clean eyeglasses

Wipe each lens with a drop of vinegar for a streak-free shine. (Don't use on plastic lenses.)

Clean book covers

Wipe with a cloth dampened in a solution of one part vinegar and two parts water.

Save a pair of scissors

Clean those sticky, grimy scissors by wiping the blades down with a cloth dampened with full-strength vinegar. Then polish to a nice gleam using a dry cloth. (Using water alone could lead to rust on the blades or the fastener holding the blades together.)

Freshen flowers

To each pint of water used, add a teaspoon each of vinegar and sugar. Will lengthen lives of fresh-cut flowers.

Get rid of gnats

In a small dish or cup, mix together equal parts apple cider vinegar and dish detergent, and set it out where the gnats are most problematic. The vinegar's sweet smell will attract them, and the dish soap will trap and kill them in the dish.

Remove smoke odors

Place a bowl of vinegar in a corner of a room to keep the room from becoming stale with cigarette smoke.

Clean deep vases

Pour a solution of vinegar and salt into the vase and let stand for an hour. Shake well and rinse thoroughly.

Brass cleaning, method 1

Mix a teaspoon of salt into a cup of vinegar. Add enough flour to make a thin paste. Rub onto the brass and allow to stand for 15 minutes. Rinse with warm water and dry to a polish.

Brass cleaning, method 2

Allow the object to soak overnight in a solution of vinegar and salt. Scrub the next morning with a brush, and wash in hot, soapy water. Rinse well.

Clean silver rings and other objects

Soak them in a solution of 1/2 cup of vinegar and 2 tablespoons of baking soda for two hours. Will make dull and dark rings look shiny and new.

Soften still paintbrushes

Boil brushes in equal parts vinegar and water for five minutes.

Get rid of paint odors

Place a small bowl of vinegar in a freshly painted room to absorb odors.

Dissolve rust from nuts and bolts

Soak the rusty objects in a bowl of full-strength vinegar overnight. Brush away residue and dry.

Clean gold jewelry

Submerge solid gold jewelry items in a cup of apple cider vinegar for 15 minutes. Then dry with a soft cloth.

OUTSIDE IDEAS

Kill grass on walks and driveways

Pour vinegar directly on unwanted grass. (Be careful not to pour on wanted plants!)

Kill weeds

Spray full strength vinegar on tops of weeds. Reapply to new growth until weeds have been starved.

Increase soil acidity

In hard-water areas, add a cup of vinegar to a gallon of tap water for watering acid-loving plants like gardenias, azaleas, or rhododendrons. The vinegar releases iron into the soil for the plants to use.

Treat plant diseases

Vinegar is useful in treating many plant diseases such as black spot, rust, and powdery mildew. Mix 2 tablespoons of apple cider vinegar in 2 quarts of water, and pour into a spray bottle. Spray the solution on your diseased plants in the morning or early evening (when temperatures are cooler and there's less direct light) until the condition is cured.

Neutralize garden lime

Rinse your hands liberally with vinegar after working with garden lime to avoid rough and flaking skin.

Keep visitors out of your garden

Soak several rags in full-strength vinegar and hang on stakes around your garden. The smell of vinegar will deter many animals, including deer, racoons, rabbits, cats, and dogs. Resoak the rags every 7 to 10 days.

Deter ants

Spray vinegar under appliances, around door and window frames, and along other known ant trails.

Bid adieu to bird droppings

Spray or pour full-strength apple cider vinegar on the poo piles and wipe up with paper towels.

Clean a hummingbird feeder

Keep those birdies coming back by keeping their feeder free from sticky, crusted-on sugar water. Clean with a solution of equal parts apple cider vinegar and hot water, using a small brush if necessary. Rinse good with cold water and allow to dry completely in the sun before adding new food.

Keep your car windows frost-free

Coat the windows the night before with a solution of three parts vinegar to one part water.

Polish car chrome

Apply full-strength vinegar with a soft cloth and polish to desired shine.

Clean car carpets

Make a solution of equal parts water and vinegar and sponge into the carpet. Wait a few minutes and then blot up with paper towels or rags. This will also remove salt residue that accumulates over the winter months.

Remove bumper stickers

Repeatedly wipe full-strength vinegar over the bumper sticker until it's saturated. Try peeling off in a few minutes. May have to reapply the vinegar.

Prolong your propane

Soak new propane lantern wicks in vinegar for several hours. Let dry before using. Will burn longer and brighter.

Clean milking equipment

Rinse with vinegar to leave system clean, disinfected and deodorized without harmful chemical residue.

Keep chickens from pecking each other

Add a splash of apple cider vinegar to their drinking water.

Clean mold and mildew off patio furniture

Spray full-strength vinegar on the affected area. The stains should wipe off easily, and the vinegar will inhibit the mildew from growing back for a while.

Clean mold and mildew off wood decks and wood furniture

In a gallon of water, mix 1 cup of ammonia, 1/2 cup of vinegar, and 1/4 cup baking soda. Brush or sponge the affected areas, rinse with cold water, and allow to dry.

KIDS AND PETS

Clean baby bottles

Soak bottles in vinegar for several hours to clean and deodorize.

Wash baby clothes and diapers

Add a cup of vinegar to the rinse cycle to break down uric acid and soap residue. Will leave clothes soft and less likely to cause a rash.

Make child's clay

Mix 2 cups of flour and a cup of salt. Stir in a teaspoon of vinegar and a 1/2 cup of water. Knead until soft. Divide into smaller portions if desired and store in refrigerator.

Make an erupting volcano

The Volcano – Combine 6 cups of flour, 2 cups of salt, 4 tablespoons of cooking oil, and 2 cups of water. Mix until smooth and firm (add more water if needed). In a four-sided baking pan (so the "lava" stays contained), place a pop bottle upright and mold the dough around it into a volcano shape. Be careful not to cover the hole or drop dough into it.

The Eruption – Fill the bottle most of the way full with warm water and a bit of red food coloring. Add 6 drops of dish detergent to the bottle. Add 2 tablespoons of baking soda next. Then slowly pour vinegar into the bottle and watch your volcano blow its top!

Remove crayon and ink marks

Using a sponge or brush, apply full-strength vinegar to the marks and rub away.

Color Easter eggs

Mix 1 teaspoon of vinegar, 1/2 cup of hot water, and food coloring in a bowl deep enough to submerge an egg.

Clean a fish tank

Vinegar works wonders on stubborn calcium deposits and coralline algae buildup. Depending on the amount of grime, use either full-strength or diluted white vinegar to scrub all areas of the tank. (A vinegar-soaked rag that's wet but not dripping works well.) Make sure to rinse with tap water afterward. Submerge small removable components in a container filled with vinegar and let them soak for a few hours. Scrub away the loosened residue and rinse thoroughly in tap water. Finally, use a vinegar spray to wipe down the outside glass.

Remove skunk odor from a dog

Rub fur with a solution of 1 cup of vinegar to 2 gallons of water. Dry off the dog but don't rinse off the solution.

Prevent fleas, ticks and mange

Add a teaspoon of vinegar to 1 quart of your pet's drinking water. Alternatively, spray a solution of equal parts vinegar and water directly on your dog's fur and rub it in. (This is a little trickier with cats. They really don't like vinegar. See next tip.)

Keep cats away

Sprinkle vinegar on those areas you don't want them walking, sleeping or scratching on.

Clean pet urine from a carpet

Apply full-strength vinegar to the affected area. Blot with cold water and let dry.

COOKING TIPS

Make a buttermilk substitute

Add a tablespoon of vinegar to a cup of milk, stir it in, and let it stand for five minutes to thicken. Instant recipe fix!

Keep strawberries fresher for longer

Put the strawberries in a large bowl. Pour water on top of them. Add a splash of vinegar and stir them around in the bowl gently. Rinse mixture off and lay them out to dry. Then place them in the refrigerator, where they will last a good two weeks thanks to the vinegar. (And no vinegar after-taste!)

Tenderize meat

For tough cuts of meat, make a marinade of 1/2 cup of vinegar (your choice as to taste) and 1 cup of heated liquid such as bouillon. Alternatively, add a tablespoon of white vinegar to your cooking liquids (for roasts, stew meats, etc.). Either way, the acetic acid in the vinegar breaks down the meat fibers, making them more tender and tasty.

Cook tastier fish

To give fish a tender, sweeter taste, soak it before cooking for 20 minutes in a mixture of 1 quart of water and 2 tablespoons of vinegar.

Freshen vegetables

Soak wilted vegetables in a quart of cold water and a tablespoon of vinegar. They'll spring up like new!

Keep potatoes white

Keep peeled potatoes from turning dark by putting them in pot of water (enough to cover) and adding 2 teaspoons of vinegar.

Make your own wine vinegar

Mix 2 tablespoons of vinegar with 1 teaspoon of dry red wine.

Replace a lemon

For normal taste buds, 1/4 teaspoon of vinegar equals 1 teaspoon of lemon juice. (Especially useful in fish recipes where you might want to cut down on odor and yet keep the taste.)

Firm up the gelatin in desserts

Add a teaspoon of vinegar for every box of gelatin used to keep those molded desserts from sagging in the summer heat.

Keep cheese longer

Wrap cheese in a vinegar-soaked cloth and keep it in a sealed container to lengthen its lifespan.

Boil better eggs

Add a tablespoon or two of vinegar to the water when boiling eggs to keep them from cracking and to allow for easier peeling.

Poach better eggs

Add a tablespoon of vinegar to the water when poaching eggs to coagulate the egg white and form a neat and compact shape to the finished product.

Prepare fluffier rice

Add a teaspoon of vinegar to the water when it boils. The rice will come out fluffier and not as sticky.

Make a simple salad dressing

Whisk together 1/4 cup of vinegar, 3/4 cup of olive oil, and a dash of Italian seasonings.

Dampen your appetite

Sprinkling a little vinegar on prepared food is said to take the edge off your appetite.

Boil better vegetables and beans

Add a teaspoon or two of vinegar to the water when boiling or steaming cauliflower, beets, and other vegetables and legumes. It will help them keep their color and reduce their gas-causing effects.

Make pasta less sticky

Add a splash of vinegar to the water as it cooks. Will also reduce the starch.

HEALTH AND HYGIENE

Relieve sunburn

Gently rub white or apple cider vinegar to skin. Apply as quickly as possible to stop the pain from getting too bad.

Condition hair

After shampooing, add a tablespoon of vinegar to your rinse to dissolve sticky residue left by shampoo.

Relieve dry and itchy skin

Add 1/2 cup of vinegar to your bath water. It will not only soften your skin, but will help keep your tub clean too.

Fight dandruff

An old folk remedy suggests warming apple cider vinegar, pouring it on the hair, and then wrapping a towel around the head. Let it set for an hour and then wash.

If you're in a hurry, an alternative method is to simply shampoo, then rinse hair with vinegar and 2 cups of warm water.

Treat acne

Make a toner of one part organic apple cider vinegar to three parts water (or more water if you have sensitive skin). After washing your face, apply the mixture to blemishes with a cotton pad and let dry naturally before putting any other creams or makeup on. Do twice a day or whenever you wash your face. (*Note: Actress Scarlett Johansson is a huge fan of using apple cider vinegar as a face wash!*)

Eliminate underarm odor

Splash on some vinegar!

Freshen your breath

Dissolve 2 tablespoons of apple cider vinegar and 1 teaspoon of salt in a glass of warm water. Rinse with this solution to get rid of onion and garlic odors.

Polish nails with ease

Before applying polish, rub fingernails with vinegar-dipped cotton balls. Cleans the nails and helps polish stay on longer.

Clean dentures

Soak dentures overnight in undiluted white vinegar. Brush and rinse in the morning.

Ease heartburn

Mix 1 tablespoon of apple cider vinegar, 1/2 teaspoon of baking soda, and a dash of sugar in a glass of water. Drink the solution about an hour after eating.

Soothe a sore throat

Mix 1 teaspoon of vinegar with a glass of water and a little honey. Gargle first, then swallow. (If you want, you can skip the honey. Also remember: no honey for children under one year old.)

Treat a raw throat

Gargle with 1 tablespoon of apple cider vinegar and 1 teaspoon of salt dissolved in a glass of warm water. Repeat several times a day if needed for a throat left raw and sore from coughing or overuse.

Breathe easier

Add 1/4 cup of vinegar to your vaporizer the next time you're congested.

Pamper your feet

Soak your feet in a solution of vinegar and warm water nightly. Your feet will soon become noticeably softer, plus it helps fight toenail fungus.

Remove warts

Mix a cup of vinegar in some warm water. Soak the wart every day for 20 minutes it disappears.

Treat psoriasis and eczema

Fill a clean squirt bottle with one part vinegar to three parts water, and spray it onto affected areas. Let air dry.

Soak aching muscles

Add two cups of apple cider vinegar to your bath water. Hey, it tenderizes meat, right?

Relieve morning sickness

Drink apple cider vinegar mixed with water and a little honey to help calm a queasy stomach.

Treat skin burns

Apply ice-cold vinegar immediately to burn for relief and to prevent blisters. (Prepare ahead of time by keeping a bottle of vinegar in the refrigerator.)

Make a vinegar elixir

A teaspoon of apple cider vinegar in a glass of water, with a bit of honey added for flavor, will take the edge off your appetite and give you an overall healthy feeling. Try it as an afternoon pickup and feel the difference!

A Word of Caution: While a teaspoon or two of apple cider vinegar is safe for most people, consult your doctor first if you are taking prescription medications, particularly diuretics and insulin, as the vinegar may interact negatively with these drugs and cause low potassium levels.

Also, don't think that just because one or two teaspoons is "good," more is better. Keep in mind that apple cider vinegar is highly acidic and could irritate your throat if taken in large quantities.

BLOOD SUGAR AND WEIGHT LOSS

Vinegar and Blood Glucose Control

The latest research shows that taking vinegar with a meal reduces the glucose response to a carbohydrate load in healthy adults as well as those suffering with type 2 diabetes. Why this works is simple: The high acetic acid content in vinegar deactivates amylase, the enzyme that turns starch into sugar. This results in less glucose being released into the blood stream. Fewer blood sugar spikes mean less insulin is needed and produced, and consequently the risk for disease progression is reduced.

In a study conducted by Arizona State University Professor Carol Johnston, at-risk and pre-diabetic adults were given two tablespoons of vinegar before lunch and dinner for 12 weeks. Their blood glucose was measured twice daily: upon waking and two hours after a meal. The end results of the study concluded that consuming vinegar at the beginning of a meal not only reduces spikes in blood sugar, but also has a favorable influence on fasting glucose concentrations.

Another recent study reported by Dr. Julian Whitaker of the Whitaker Wellness Institute found that when diabetic adults were given two tablespoons of apple cider vinegar (mixed with water and a noncaloric sweetener) right before a high-carbohydrate meal consisting of a bagel and orange juice, their glucose and insulin response was dramatically lowered.

In fact, according to Dr. Whitaker, "Vinegar worked just as well as diabetes drugs and reduced the usual blood sugar surge in people with diabetes and insulin resistance (pre-diabetes) by 25 percent and 50 percent, respectively, and improved insulin sensitivity 19 percent and 34 percent."

While these findings are encouraging for people looking for alternative or supplemental ways to manage their blood sugar, experts stress that if you're already on diabetes medication, don't try to substitute vinegar for it until you talk to your doctor. Some people can't tolerate the ingestion of vinegar, and some have other problems related to diabetes (such as gastro paresis) that vinegar can actually make worse.

If you don't have these pre-existing conditions, a common recommendation is to take two to four teaspoons of vinegar before or with your meals to reduce blood sugar levels. And no, you don't have to drink it straight. (Please don't! It could burn your esophagus or make you nauseous.) Here are some easy, tasty ways to get your daily dose of vinegar:

- Use a vinegar and oil dressing on your salads. Just be careful not to use a fruity or sweet vinegar; white, apple cider, balsamic, and red wine are all good choices. Also make sure your dressing is at least 50 to 75 percent vinegar. Add some Italian seasonings, minced garlic, or Dijon mustard for additional flavoring.

- Drizzle vinaigrette (or whatever dressing you just made for your salads) over steamed and roasted vegetables, such as cauliflower, broccoli, asparagus, and green beans.

- Dip your bread into a mixture of vinegar and olive oil (two parts vinegar to one part oil). Be careful of the type of bread you use, as many grains will make blood sugar rise significantly. Sourdough is an excellent choice, as it contains a substance brought about by its fermentation process that tempers blood sugar levels.

- Marinate your meat and fish in vinegar. It is a natural tenderizer anyway, so your meat will come out tender, tasty, and moist.

- Eat pickles and other pickled vegetables with your meals. Korean kimchi and German sauerkraut, for example, are good vinegar-rich vegetable side dishes.

- Make a drinkable tonic by mixing 1-2 tablespoons of apple cider vinegar with 8 oz. of water. Add a non-caloric sweetener if you like. Sip before, during, and after your meal.

Finally, remember that the key to vinegar's success in reducing blood sugar spikes is the fact that it works against starch, not refined sugar. So in other words, it will help if you eat bread or pasta, but not candy or cake.

Vinegar and Weight Control

Can vinegar help you lose weight? The answer is . . . *perhaps*.

As I've just discussed, current research clearly demonstrates that vinegar helps control the glycemic effect of carbohydrate-laden meals. Now, in weight loss circles it is pretty widely acknowledged that a low-glycemic diet often results in weight loss. So a logical deduction would be that, yes, vinegar can help you lose weight since it induces a lower-GI effect.

The fact that vinegar acts as an appetite suppressant and slows gastric emptying are further reasons perhaps that many people have had success losing weight when adding more vinegar to their diet. A study published in 2005 seems to back this up. Participants who were given vinegar with a high-carbohydrate breakfast (again bagels and orange juice) not only saw a reduction in their blood sugar surge post-meal, but ate on average 200 fewer calories the rest of the day than those who didn't have the vinegar.

A more recent study undertaken in Japan considered the effect of apple cider vinegar on 175 overweight men and women. The participants were divided into two groups: one group was given a daily drink containing 1-2 tablespoons of apple cider vinegar. The other group was given no vinegar. After twelve weeks the daily vinegar group had significantly lower body weight, BMI, visceral fat, and waist circumference than the no-vinegar group.

Dr. Jason Fung, in his book *The Obesity Code: Unlocking the Secrets of Weight Loss*, reports that when potatoes were served cold and dressed with vinegar, they induced a considerably lower glycemic response than regular potatoes. In fact, both glycemic and insulin index levels were reduced by 43 percent and 31 percent respectively. Cooked and cooled potatoes (as well as raw) are known to contain high levels of resistant starch, which studies have shown lower blood glucose levels and improve insulin sensitivity. When vinegar is added to the mix, the benefit is even greater. As Dr. Fung further explains: "Vinegar does not displace the carbohydrate, but actually seems to exert a protective effect on the serum insulin response."

While there are few definitive scientific studies out there that directly target the correlation between vinegar and weight loss, there are plenty of anecdotal weight loss results that have come about from other studies examining vinegar's effects on cholesterol, appetite suppression, and fat deposits.

Case in point: In 2004, Dr. Carol Johnston, a nutrition professor at the Arizona State University, conducted a study to examine the effects of vinegar on cholesterol levels. While Johnston found the vinegar to have no effect on lowering cholesterol, she did discover, unintentionally, that those who ingested a tablespoon of vinegar before lunch and dinner lost an average of two pounds over four weeks. (And this was accomplished during the holiday months of November and December.)

Dr. Julian Whitaker on his website reports of a study wherein individuals were instructed to take two tablespoons of vinegar before two of their daily meals for four weeks. In addition to experiencing reductions in their blood glucose levels, they lost an average of two pounds, and some as much as four during that time frame. This result caused researchers to speculate that vinegar may interfere with enzymes that break down carbohydrates, thus allowing carbohydrates to pass through the body without being absorbed.

In 2005, a study conducted by Swedish researcher Dr. Elin Ostman found participants to be less hungry a couple of hours after eating bread with vinegar as opposed to eating bread alone. Folklorists have long maintained that vinegar acts as an appetite suppressant (and therefore a weight loss aid). Science now seems to corroborate this.

A 2009 Japanese study was conducted on mice in which one group of mice was fed a high-fat diet and acetic acid (the main component in vinegar), and another group of mice was fed the same diet but given water instead of acetic acid. After six weeks, the mice in the acetic acid group had 10% less body fat than the mice in the water group.

Japanese researchers believe that the acetic acid in vinegar activates genes that produce proteins that in turn help the body break down fats. Such an action helps prevent fat buildup and thus helps guard against weight gain.

Dr. Johnston attributes these results to another unique function of acetic acid. She describes acetic acid as basically a starch and sugar blocker. It inhibits the activity of various carbohydrate-digesting enzymes, such as amylase, sucrase, maltase, and lactase. When these enzymes are blocked, sugars and starches pass through the digestive tract much the way that indigestible fiber does.

Much more research is needed to definitively proclaim vinegar as a weight loss wonder, despite the claims of many fad diet proponents and books. But given its proven effect on blood glucose, tempering the glycemic load of carbohydrate-rich meals, appetite suppression, and key metabolic processes, it only seems natural to include it in one's daily health regime.

Did you catch that key word? *Natural*. Vinegar is all that and more.

Last Words

Needless to say, this compilation is by no means exhaustive. Perhaps after reading through, you've come up with some of your own ideas for using vinegar, based on your personal needs. After all, if vinegar can, say, deodorize a lunchbox, maybe it can also deodorize your . . . (fill in the blank). Feel free to experiment. The secret to mastering household tasks, obtaining better health, and keeping the planet greener is only a bottle away!

ACKNOWLEDGEMENTS

A myriad of resources was consulted in compiling this compendium of vinegar lore and facts. While too numerous and impractical to list individually, the author would like to offer a special acknowledgement to The Vinegar Institute, an international trade association representing the vast majority of vinegar manufacturers and bottlers. The Vinegar Institute is an invaluable source for all things vinegar, and especially for keeping up on the latest research news and market trends.

The author would also like to acknowledge the following sources for the information used in the discussions of glucose control and weight loss:

Brand-Miller, Jennie. "Q & A With Professor Jennie Brand-Miller." Glycemic Index Foundation Newsletter. March 2016.

Breakstone, Stephanie. "Metabolism Booster! Vinegar." Prevention.com. 3 November 2011.

Challem, Jack. "A Spoonful of Vinegar Helps the Blood Sugar Go Down." Dlife.com. 23 June 2011.

Fung, Jason. *The Obesity Code: Unlocking the Secrets of Weight Loss*. 2016.

Johnston, Carol S., and Cindy A. Gass. "Vinegar: Medicinal Uses and Antiglycemic Effect." Medscape.com. 30 May 2006.

Johnston, Carol S., Samantha Quagliano, and Serena Whit. "Thereputic Effect of Daily Vinegar Ingestion For Individuals At Risk For Type 2 Diabetes." The FASEB Journal 27.1 Supplement (2013): 1079-56.

Kondo, Tomoo, et al. "Acetic Acid Upregulates the Expression of Genes for Fatty Acid Oxidation Enzymes in Liver To Suppress Body Fat Accumulation." Journal of Agricultural and Food Chemistry, 2009, 57 (13), pp 5982–5986.

Mercola, Joseph. "How Apple Cider Vinegar Can Change Your Life." Mercola.com. 21 March 2015.

Ostman E, Granfeldt Y, Persson L, et al. "Vinegar Supplementation Lowers Glucose and Insulin Responses and Increases Satiety After a Bread Meal in Healthy Subjects." European Journal of Clinical Nutrition, 2005, 59, 983-988.

Samad, Anuar, Azrina Azlan, and Amin Ismail. "Therapeutic Effects of Vinegar: A Review." Current Opinion in Food Science 8 (2016): 56-61.

ABOUT THE AUTHOR

M.B. Ryther is a freelance writer whose work has appeared in a variety of print and online magazines, including *Country Woman*, *Mother Earth News*, *Woman's World*, *Catholic Digest*, *L.A. Parent*, and *Boys' Life*. She lives in eastern Washington with her husband and children.

.

Printed in Great Britain
by Amazon